borborygmic roars
culverin

To step
To slew
bracken
panniered
scurf
soothering

94 - The Train
44 from Europa And The Bull

√√ The Swan 82
Stormy Night 80

√√. Ireland 40

√√√ The Net 78

√√√√ Autumn Day 92

92 — Took the hook of the mind and
reeled out the eye's line / into
whips and whirl-spools of light,
when every ash-shoot shone

Gallery Books
Editor: Peter Fallon

POEMS
W. R. Rodgers

W. R. Rodgers

POEMS

*Edited and introduced
by Michael Longley*

Gallery Books

Poems
is first published
simultaneously in paperback
and in a clothbound edition
on 30 June 1993.

The Gallery Press
Loughcrew
Oldcastle
County Meath
Ireland

ISBN 1 85235 106 3 (*paperback*)
    1 85235 107 1 (*clothbound*)

The Gallery Press receives financial assistance from An Chomhairle Ealaíon / The Arts Council, Ireland, and acknowledges also the assistance of the Arts Council of Northern Ireland in the publication of this book.

Contents

Preface

The text printed here follows the Secker & Warburg editions of *Awake! and Other Poems* (1941) and *Europa and the Bull and Other Poems* (1952). *Collected Poems* was published by Oxford University Press in 1971 and contains ten uncollected poems as well as the unfinished 'Epilogue to "The Character of Ireland"'. I have followed *Collected Poems* for the text of the last six pieces in this book. In the interests of balance I have taken the liberty of cutting 'Europa and the Bull', and I include only the main part of 'Epilogue'. *Europa and the Bull*'s dedicatory poem, 'To M.', is placed at the front of this selection. (M. is Marianne, Rodgers' second wife.) In order to suggest the poet's development, as I sense it, and to highlight his finest achievements I have slightly rearranged the poems, keeping in mind three principles: Rodgers' original order, theme, and appearance on the page.

Only two 'new' poems have turned up: 'Herod's Story' and 'Prologue to the Countess Cathleen'. Although neither is in this selection, both deserve to be considered when eventually an annotated *Collected Poems* is being prepared. I am grateful to Douglas Carson for showing me these, and for his sound advice, useful information and generous assistance. Mr Carson is preparing for publication an edition of *The Return Room*, Rodgers' brilliant radio feature about his Belfast childhood. The poet's daughter Lucy Rodgers Cohen is making a compilation of the many unpublished prose pieces. She and Rodgers' step-daughter Nina Hutchison have criticised my introduction most helpfully.

In writing my introduction I have found the following essays and articles useful and interesting: 'W. R. Rodgers: Romantic Calvinist' by Terence Brown (in *Northern Voices*, 1975); '"The Dissidence of Dissent": John Hewitt and W. R. Rodgers' by John Wilson Foster (in *Colonial Consequences*, 1991); 'The Fate of "Identity": John Hewitt, W. R. Rodgers and Louis MacNeice' by Peter McDonald (in the *Irish Review*, No. 12); Dan Davin's memoir which introduces *Collected Poems*; and the *Honest Ulsterman*'s 'W. R. Rodgers Supplement', edited by Tom Clyde, with criticism and biography by Gerald Dawe, Michael O'Neill, Douglas

Carson and Tom Clyde (No. 92). For biographical information I have relied heavily on Darcy O'Brien's *W. R. Rodgers* (1970) in the Bucknell University Press's *Irish Writers Series*.

Introduction

In the graveyard of Cloveneden Church in Loughgall,
County Armagh, W. R. Rodgers is commemorated on his
headstone as Poet and Preacher. Ulster is still likely to
produce poets who write out of a response to religion. Like
his friend Louis MacNeice, Rodgers was motivated by
strong anti-puritan feelings. The vividness they share was
projected partly as an assault on religious narrowness and
cultural restriction. Rodgers was born in Belfast in 1909, the
son of respectable Presbyterian parents. Intensely religious
and, in the Ulster phrase, 'good living', they banned
alcohol, tobacco, dancing, theatre-going and full-length
mirrors. 'Sunday dinner was cooked on Saturday, and the
Sunday boots were polished the night before, and profane
books and music were put away till Monday, and nothing,
absolutely nothing, was allowed to disturb "the Day of
Dreadful Rest", as we restless children called it.' In his
pioneering essay 'W. R. Rodgers: Romantic Calvinist'
Terence Brown argues that 'the intense pressure suggested
by Rodgers' verbal practices exist[s] . . . because of, not in
spite of, the repressive constrictions of his early experience'.
Though Rodgers came from a strict Calvinist family and
suffered in childhood from Old Dissent puritanism, his
cultural background was neither threadbare nor tongue-
tied. In his radio feature *The Return Room*, which was first
broadcast in 1955, he recreates his early childhood in
Belfast:

> There was a halo of hills round me from the start, and a
> hug-me-tight of holiness. All the pubs held their breath
> that day, and the bells of the city danced with their hands
> in their pockets, and the soothering river ran wild, and a
> decorated tramcar took over the hills and far way. My
> father, who had a fine sense of occasion — "We may put a
> nick in the post today!" — my father got down the Good
> Book and read from the roll of the generations of great
> men: ' . . . Enos which was the son of Seth which was the
> son of Adam which was the son of God'.

In July the family would rent a holiday cottage in the countryside at Carryduff, not far from Belfast. 'The duck twirled like a stick on the stream, each gay cloud was off on its own, the very clod sang. Apart from my enemy, the nettle, there was only one flaw to it all.' He is referring to the Plymouth Brethren's gospel tents which descended 'on our fields like pentecostal tongues, and the reapers of souls cut swathes of hymns through the standing silence'. The boy longed to be back in Belfast for the more raucous celebrations of the Twelfth of July, 'to hear the dreadful thunder of the big Orange drums' and 'to see the Kingly-painted walls, and the wonderful rafts of rivering flags winding through the streets of the windfall city':

> *There would be a bonfire in our back street that night. It would light up the roses on the wall-paper of the return room. It would flicker on the picture of Robbie Burns. It would glimmer on the tallboy with its deep drawers full of treasures — a black silk topper, a purple Edwardian waistcoat with lace on it, a copy of the Solemn League and Covenant, a Volunteer hat that looked like a cowboy's, a silver sovereign-case. The bonfire would redden it all; even the still little Georgian mirror would go wig-wag in the glare of it. How long would it be, I reflected, before my farthing face would grow to a crown? And would I ever be able to see myself, all of myself? For there was no full-length mirror in our Puritan house. Such a thing would have been an abomination, a sin in excelsis, for it might get too enamoured of a person.*

After receiving his B.A. with honours in English at Queen's University in 1931, Rodgers entered the Presbyterian Theological College to prepare for the ministry. The *Armagh Standard* reported his ordination on 18 January 1935. The sermon was preached by the Reverend R. G. Fry of Ahorey:

> *You may take it that your minister, like every other minister, will be 'a man of sorrows and acquainted with grief'. He can only teach you what he has learned himself, and if*

on any Sabbath Day . . . he seems to speak with unusual
power, be sure that he paid a great price for that freedom.
He got it through the furnace. The foundations are laid in
tears and blood.

The *Armagh Standard* also recorded how later at the manse
Rodgers introduced himself to his parishioners: 'There were
one thousand and one influences working upon his life in
bringing him to that day . . . . He was animated with a desire
to do his part in the ingathering of Christ's Kingdom . . . .
He could only pray that he might be worthy of his hopes and
inspirations . . . . He came that day as their minister and
teacher, and yet he had many things to learn from them.' He
describes his ministry in an unpublished essay: 'A rural
community is a close and intricate wickerwork of human
relationships and functions . . . . The role I was called to fill
was that of parson and, being young, I found it a formidable
one. Old men, full of worldly experience, farmers who
never hesitated to advise me on practical matters, would at
once defer to me, as sons to a father, when it came to other-
worldly matters and spiritual crises. Not that they were
impressed by my personal authority; authority for them
resided in the role and office which I happened to occupy
. . . I realised that I, as an individual, did not matter, and this
in a way was a relief to me as well as an instruction.' In many
respects an unorthodox clergyman, Rodgers is still remembered affectionately in Loughgall for reserving part of every
sermon for the children; and for the broad sympathies
which gained him the title 'the Catholic Presbyterian'.
   In 1936 he married Marie Harden Waddell whom he
had first met when he was studying for the ministry and she
was a medical student at Queen's. In his monograph
on Rodgers, Darcy O'Brien describes their relationship
sympathetically. 'Her physical and intellectual vitality
seemed complementary to his diffident and rather dreamy
nature . . . . With her, he might learn to be more at home in
the world. With him, her bright rationalism might soften
under his lyrical sense of the mystery of things. A year after
his ordination, he brought her to his parish . . . . She was to
be the village physician. While he was ministering to the

souls of his flock, she would look after their bodies.' The niece of Rutherford Mayne the playwright and of Helen Waddell the scholar and translator of medieval Latin poetry, she was herself an unfulfilled writer. A son was stillborn; but in 1939 their first daughter Harden was born, and in 1941 Nini. The marriage did not prosper, and Marie became mentally ill, subject to fits of depression. In O'Brien's account 'each became the other's best enemy and, to retreat, they drank, so their rows became drunken ones'. He strove to carry on his ministry and to shield Marie and himself in a small community. In 'Paired Lives' husband and wife present, like swing doors, 'one smooth front / Of summed resistance', but the reality is different:

> *Each singly yields to thrust,*
> *Is hung on its own hinge*
> *Of fear and hope, and in*
> *Its own reticence rests.*

As a poet Rodgers was a late starter. In 1938, three years after his ordination, his friend John Hewitt lent him books by contemporary poets, of whom Auden made the biggest impact. Poems came steadily after that. By 1940 the thirty-two lyrics he had written to that date were collected in *Awake! and Other Poems*. The first printing was destroyed by the blitz on Plymouth, but the publishers brought out a second printing in 1941, and an American edition appeared in 1942. In John Hewitt's generous account 'the reviews were enthusiastic and the poet's reputation was made. Rooted in the landscape of Armagh and the Mournes and given their mood by the European war, the volume presented a new poet with an exuberant vocabulary and a subtle sensory awareness.' In an interesting prefatory note to *Awake!* Rodgers describes his own position and at the same time pinpoints some of the problems which may face a provincial poet:

> *That this volume contains all the poems I have so far*
> *written is not an accident; that none was written earlier*
> *than three years ago is not without meaning; for I was*

*schooled in a backwater of literature out of sight of the
running stream of contemporary verse. Some murmurs of
course I heard, but I was singularly ignorant of its extent
and character. It was in the late thirties that I came to
contemporary poetry, and I no longer stood dumb in the
tied shops of speech or felt stifled in the stale air of conven-
tion.*

After this emotional thaw Rodgers' language flowed in
headlong spate. He was taken over by 'the arriving winds of
words' and remained 'their most astonished host'. His view
of poetry and inspiration is pentecostal. The reader is struck
by the tumble of words and images, the puns, the risky
deployment of colloquialism and cliché, the rich, idiosyn-
cratic vocabulary, the out-of-the-way associations and
juxtapositions, and the alliterative music which is usually
attributed to the influence of Gerard Manley Hopkins. John
Hewitt puts us right: 'Superficial critics insist on his deriva-
tion from Hopkins, whereas the fact is . . . that the greater
body of his book, *Awake! and Other Poems*, was written
before he had read that infectious Jesuit.' And he directs to
James Joyce 'those who wish to detect the element of Irishry
in him'. He shares with his contemporaries Dylan Thomas
and George Barker a linguistic and rhythmic ebullience, a
tendency towards excess. Rodgers himself suggests that 'the
faculty of standing words or ideas on their heads — by
means of pun, epigram, bull, or what-have-you — is a
singularly Irish one . . . . To the English ear, which likes
understatement, it is all rather excessive and therefore not
quite in good taste. But to the Irish mind, which likes
gesture, bravado, gallivanting, and rhetoric, it is an accept-
able tradition.' But even to an Irish mind, surely, Rodgers
throughout his career often goes over the top. 'Nothing
pleases me so much in writing as to be able to sit on both
sides of the sense, and if there were six sides I would sit on
them all.' In his essay 'The Dissidence of Dissent' John
Wilson Foster suggests that his 'liberties, abandonments and
superfluous energies might be laid at the door of a trans-
posed evangelical fervour'. The preacher has not yet been
subsumed in the poet who, like a diminutive John Bunyan,

allows personified abstractions to clump through his lines. One such is 'Contempt the caretaker' who rather spoils 'The Party'. In Kathleen Raine's opinion Rodgers 'is never dull, never flat — except when he has something to say of a philosophic nature, when he drops into bathos'.

Beneath the celebrations there sounds a grumbling ground bass, 'ratchets of agitation', as though the light of poetry is too bright for eyes grown accustomed to 'the darkened house', the manse. 'It was always afternoon in my parish, the full tide of sleep brimming the sky; the shot bird hung in the air, the blown rose refused to fall, the clock stood still.' Obsessive images of entrapment recur — nets, thongs, ropes, webs, threads. The poet, 'listening for the fat click of the softly-shut door', feels threatened in his private life and by external circumstance:

> *I shouted and none answered, one by one*
> *My listening hopes crept back to me*
> *Out of that dead place; mine was a lighted face*
> *Looking into darkness, seen, but seeing nothing.*

'These early poems are,' Terence Brown suggests, 'the work of a personality at war with itself, torn between the Calvinist's sense of duty and responsibility, and a romantic's need for a rich diversity and profusion of experience.' Claustrophobia shades into paranoia. In 'Beagles' he identifies with 'the little and elastic hare' pursued by 'the whole blind world'. The hunters' shouts turn into 'A tether that held me to the hare / Here, there and everywhere'. The first book tests possibilities of change and escape. He refers again and again to boundaries, borders, edges, rims, the horizon. One of his poems about the war is called 'Escape':

> *. . . You will be more free*
> *At the thoughtless centre of slaughter than you would be*
> *Standing chained to the telephone-end while the world*
> *cracks.*

Also at the end of his tether, exhausted after writing and producing seventy programmes in four years, Louis

tion, 'Lent', in which Jesus is reborn in the womb of Mary Magdalene once she has relented and allowed her lenten mask of self-denial to thaw. In return for her warmth Christ returns to her the emblems of her sensuality:

> Dance, Mary Magdalene, dance, dance and sing,
> For unto you is born
> This day a King. 'Lady,' said He,
> 'To you who relent
> I bring back the petticoat and the bottle of scent.'

This magnificent poem gathers around itself several other original meditations and celebrations: 'The Trinity'; 'Carol' which is perfect; 'Resurrection' in which the voice of authority rings out over two hundred and sixty lines as Rodgers like a modern Saint Paul rethinks and feels afresh the Easter story; 'Nativity' and 'The Journey of the Magi', overlong and flawed, but, in their best moments, rich and generous:

> It was the child within themselves
> For which they'd sought, for which Age delves
> — Now Age and Innocence can meet,
> Now, now the circle is complete,
> The journey's done. Lord, Lord, how sweet!

What other poet brings the reader closer to the Jesus who washed the feet of the disciples; who 'figured it forth / In the breaking of bread'; who conceived 'The Lord's Prayer' and 'The Sermon on the Mount'? As in 'Nativity' ('His holly hair, his berry eyes are here, / And his chrysanthemum wound, / This Christmas day . . . '), so in 'Christ Walking on the Water' Rodgers portrays Jesus the man, his doubt and despair, his naturalness, his earthiness, his sexuality, and thereby his greatness:

> . . . he like a lover, caught up,
> Pushed past all wrigglings and remonstrances
> And entered the rolling belly of the boat
> That shuddered and lay still. And he lay there
> Emptied of his errand, oozing still . . .

Christ is at once an omnipotent god — 'the hub, / Both bone and flesh, finger and ring of all / This clangorous sea' — and a bewildered man. At the end of the poem he slumps down in the boat, agitated and exhausted, 'His knees drawn up, his head dropped deep, / Curled like a question mark asleep'. In his review of *Europa and the Bull* G. S. Fraser writes of Rodgers' 'sacramentalisation of sex'. At moments of great intensity religious and sexual experiences seem for this poet to be one and the same. The inspiration behind these remarkable pieces was his affair, lasting seven years, with Marianne Gilliam, whom he had first met in 1945. She was the wife of his immediate boss, Laurence Gilliam, Head of the Features Department in the BBC. 'The Net', one of the most passionate love poems in the language, is addressed to her. The anatomical hard facts have seldom been conveyed with such fierce precision and loving care:

Quick, woman, in your net
Catch the silver I fling!
O I am deep in your debt,
Draw tight, skin-tight, the string,
And rake the silver in.
No fisher ever yet
Drew such a cunning ring.

Rodgers' wife, Marie, held a number of positions in Scottish hospitals, but she never completely regained her health. She died in Newcastle, County Down, in 1953. Rodgers crossed to Ireland for the funeral. In the same year he married Marianne. O'Brien quotes Laurence Gilliam as saying: 'She may make him happy, but he will not write any more poetry.' In 1956 their daughter Lucy was born. *Collected Poems* which was published in 1971, two years after his death in America, contains a further ten pieces (plus the never-to-be-completed 'Epilogue'), the rather disappointing harvest of sixteen years. At the BBC he invented a form of radio collage — known as 'the Rodgers method' — which is now taken for granted. By carefully editing and cross-cutting interviews with and about Irish writers he produced a series of portraits (published in 1972 by the BBC

levity and fireworks', he also knows that

> ... *the god has always a foot of clay, and the soul*
> *Grows in soil, the flower has a dark root.*

Michael Longley
Belfast, September 1992

Words

Always the arriving winds of words
Pour like Atlantic gales over these ears,
These reefs, these foils and fenders, these shrinking
And sea-scalded edges of the brain-land.
Rebutted and rebounding, on they post
Past my remembrance, falling all unplanned.
But some day out of darkness they'll come forth,
Arrowed and narrowed into my tongue's tip,
And speak for me — their most astonished host.

The Lovers

After the tiff there was stiff silence, till
One word, flung in centre like single stone,
Starred and cracked the ice of her resentment
To its edge. From that stung core opened and
Poured up one outward and widening wave
Of eager and extravagant anger.

The Party

So they went, leaving a picnic-litter of talk
And broken glitter of jokes, the burst bags of spite:
In comes Contempt the caretaker, eye on ceiling,
Broom in armpit, and with one wide careless cast
Sweeps the stuttering rubbish out of memory,
Opens the shutters, puts out the intimate lamp,
And, a moment, gazes on the mute enormities
Of distant dawn. And far doors bang in mind, idly.

War-time

Now all our hurries that hung up on hooks,
And all our heels that idly kicked in halls,
And all our angers that at anchor swung,
And all our youth long tethered to dole-lines,
And all our roots that rotted deep in dump,
Are recollected: in country places
Old men gather the children round them now,
As an old tree, when lopped of every bough,
Gathers the young leaves into itself, a frilled stump.

Escape

The roads of Europe are running away from the war,
Running fast over the mined bridges and past the men
Waiting there, with watch, ready to maim and arrest them,
And strong overhead the long snorings of the planes' tracks
Are stretching like rafters from end to end of their power.
Turn back, you who want to escape or want to forget
The ruin of all your regards. You will be more free
At the thoughtless centre of slaughter than you would be
Standing chained to the telephone-end while the world cracks.

The Interned Refugee

And I was left here in the darkened house,
Listening for the fat click of the softly-shut door,
Looking for the oiled glint and ghost of light
Sliding soundlessly along the wall toward me,
Knowing that round me They were mobilising
Their cold implacable forces slowly.

I shouted and none answered, one by one
My listening hopes crept back to me
Out of that dead place; mine was a lighted face
Looking into darkness, seen, but seeing nothing.

An Irish Lake

There in the hard light
Dark birds, pink-footed, dab and pick
Among the addery roots and marrowy stones,
And the blown waves blink and hiccup at the lake's
Lip. A late bee blares and drones on inland
Into a cone-point of silence, and I
Lying at the rhododendron's foot
Look through five fingers' grille at the lake
Shaking, at the bare and backward plain, and
The running and bending hills that carry
Like a conveyor belt the bright snail-line
Of clouds along the sky all day unendingly.

There, far from the slack noose of rumour
That tightens into choking fact, I relax,
And sounds and sights and scents sail slowly by.
But suddenly, like delicate and tilted italics,
The up-standing birds stretch urgently away
Into the sky as suddenly grown grey.
Night rounds on Europe now. And I must go.
Before its hostile faces peer and pour
Over the mind's rim enveloping me,
And my so-frightened thoughts dart here and there
Like trout among their grim stony gazes.

Summer Day

But, heedful of the man who walks alone
On the dunes now at noon, in the heat here
At the sightless bottom of a sand-bowl
Two lovers hesitate, stop, looking up
At the single eye of sky vacantly
Accusing them, at the stiffened lashes
Of grasses circling it. But nothing moves.
And they again resume their easy grooves.

Stormy Day

O look how the loops and balloons of bloom
Bobbing on long strings from the finger-ends
And knuckles of the lurching cherry-tree
Heap and hug, elbow and part, this wild day,
Like a careless carillon cavorting;
And the beaded whips of the beeches splay
And dip like anchored weed round a drowned rock,
And hovering effortlessly the rooks
Hang on the wind's effrontery as if
On hooks, then loose their hold and slide away
Like sleet sidewards down the warm swimming sweep
Of wind. O it is a lovely time when
Out of the sunk and rigid sumps of thought
Our hearts rise and race with new sounds and sights
And signs, tingling delightedly at the sting
And crunch of springless carts on gritty roads,
The caught kite dangling in the skinny wires,
The swipe of a swallow across the eyes,
Striped awnings stretched on lawns. New things surprise
And stop us everywhere. In the parks
The fountains scoop and flower like rockets
Over the oval ponds whose even skin
Is pocked and goosefleshed by their niggling rain
That frocks a naked core of statuary.
And at jetty's jut, roped and ripe for hire,
The yellow boats lie yielding and lolling,
Jilted and jolted like jellies. But look!
There! Do you see, crucified on palings,
Motionless news-posters announcing
That now the frozen armies melt and meet

And smash? Go home now, for, try as you may,
You will not shake off that fact today.
Behind you limps that dog with tarry paw,
As behind him, perfectly timed, follows
The dumb shadow that mimes him all the way.

Ireland

O these lakes and all gills that live in them,
These acres and all legs that walk on them,
These tall winds and all wings that cling to them,
Are part and parcel of me, bit and bundle,
Thumb and thimble. Them I am, but none more
Than the mountains of Mourne that turn and trundle
Roundly like slow coils of oil along the shore
Of Down and on inland. When I begin
To draw my memory's nets and outlines in,
Then through its measured mesh escapes the fuss
And fluster of all the finicky things.
Of the Mournes I remember most the mist,
The grey granite goosefleshed, the minute
And blazing parachutes of fuchsia, and us
Listening to the tiny clustered clinks
Of little chisels tinkling tirelessly
On stone, like a drip of birds' beaks picking
Rapidly at scattered grain. I think of those
Wet sodden days when we, for miles and miles,
Steadily padded the slow sponge of turf
That squealed and squelched cold between our bared toes;
Or on airy ridge, urgent and agile, ran,
A chain of jigging figures on the sky-line;
Or, skilfully in file, followed, tricking
The hoops of hairy bramble in our path,
Poking in undergrowth and picking
The bitter berries that prickle the springs
Of the dark mouth. There was Bloody River
Where the granite pickles bristled and blazed, and
Ebullient water bellied over

Boulders with the sweep of a bell's shoulders,
And pancaked out in pools: Drinihilla
Where the gales smoothed and glued back the eyelids:
The granite river that is called Kilkeel,
Whose beds were clean and gritty like oatmeal:
And Commedagh in whose high summer heat
Nothing stirred, only the shimmering bleat
Of sheep; and we, as we sat and chattered,
Marked the motionless shine of falls far-off
On Binyon, and nothing at all mattered:
And Legawherry so soft and grassy,
Where the white scuts lazily scattered,
And never in their remotest burrows
Did ferret-Fear come closely after them:
Slieve-na-brock and its long pig-tail trickles
That hung down the bald rocks, reaching to
The glossy backs of the bracken. And Donard
Where, high over all hanging, the strong hawk
Held in his eyes whole kingdoms, sources, seas,
And in his foot-hooks felt all things wriggling
Like the single string of river niggling
Among the enormous mountain bottoms.
Bearnagh and Lamigan and Chimney-Rock,
Spelga, Pulgarve, and Cove — all these names lie
Silently in my grass-grown memory,
Each one bright and steady as a frog's eye;
But touch it and it leaps, leaps like a bead
Of mercury that breaks and scatters
Suddenly in a thousand shining strings
And running spools and ever-dwindling rings
Round the mind's bowl, till at last all drop,
Lumped and leaden again, to one full stop.

The Fountains

Suddenly all the fountains in the park
Opened smoothly their umbrellas of water,
Yet there was none but me to miss or mark
Their peacock show, and so I moved away
Uneasily, like one who at a play
Finds himself all alone, and will not stay.

Life's Circumnavigators

Here, where the taut wave hangs
Its tented tons, we steer
Through rocking arch of eye
And creaking reach of ear,
Anchored to flying sky,
And chained to changing fear.

O when shall we, all spent,
Row in to some far strand,
And find, to our content,
The original land
From which our boat once went,
Though not the one we planned.

Us on that happy day
This fierce sea will release,
On our rough face of clay,
The final glaze of peace.
Our oars we all will lay
Down, and desire will cease.

from Europa and the Bull

Naked they came, a niggling core of girls
Maggoting gaily in the curling wool
Of morning mist, and careless as the lark
That gargled overhead. They were the root
Of all that writhing air, the frothing rock
Of that grey sea in whose vacuity
Footless they stood, nor knew if it or they
Were moving now. Yet, even as they gazed,
Cave after cave of light calved out of gloom,
Roof rose on roof, laugh laddered into laugh
As on they glided through the muddling veils
Into the motionless meadow, clear as stone,
Interminably domed.
Nothing supernal here; only cow-parsley:
Any place was convenient velvet,
And everywhere was peace, pin-drizzled by
Bird-song; the bay bare like a gong
Unbruised. Easy at the sea's edge the rocks
Breathed up and down. The inland hills stood still
Like hoardings to be stared at. Happy place!
And happy happy day! How giddily then
They sleeked along the sand with smoking heels.
Some frayed off with fountain-fling of arms
To play and plunge, staccatoing the water
And some more slowly followed, picking the deep flowers
Out of the fume and underdrone of bees: green-kneed
They rose and fell in waves delightedly: new sights
Consumed them; new mites and motes of smell
Held and incensed them: crumbs of booty glowed
In every foot-dent, eiderdowntrodden.

And all among them moved the moon-like cows
Grazing light tracks across the long night-grass.
But look! the Bull! Indubitably bull,
Elbowing slowly through the obeisant herd,
Blazing and bellowing. His massy head,
Laden like a dahlia, dallied and swung,
And his vast eye slid to and fro as sharp
And glaucous as sea-holly, salting all
Their thoughts with suddenness. They hardly knew
What most to admire: but most his hub of power
And circumambience of gentleness
Delighted them. Arms curved and craved to stroke
His milky sides, insidiously veined
With watery blues and bloody ivyings.
But how describe him? words can only add
To lightning the thunder's redundancy.
He was most godlike and most temperate.

Slow, slow, slow, with bubble-pause and slide
He paced before Europa there, and she
As if with shivering drew her shoulders now
Shyly about her, yet she shivered still.
Never did shadow so shimmer with midges
As she with switherings. Should she go?
Or no? Body and soul see-sawed in her.
As slowly the swan comes forward, in advance
Bearing its bellying tray of effusive plumes,
Yet backward rears its head and huffs its glance
As if it fended off its offering that presumes:
Swollen with slowness and undertowed by longing
It grows on the water, close, thundery, and thronging,
Till suddenly beside us, without fuss,
Immense it blossoms like a cumulus —
So slowly rose Europa, slowly she

Opened her fan-like self and mounted him
And spread her valances.
O how his reticence reined and trounced him then,
Lifting his feet into flounces of flight
And ratchet-edges of agitation,
Chawing each gentle step. To have and to hold —
How he would love to have but feared to hold
Her who as smooth as metal sat and smiled.
And how his silver slaverings flowed, and now
His chattering hooves danced under him like stones.

　　　　　　　　No one noticed
The Bull and Europa sloping away
Westward into the weed, she with both hands
Holding her bellyful of jolted joy,
Buoyant but dubious: he, bushed in stealth,
Tiptoadying tenderly, picking his way
Between brusque grass and briar, till at last
He waded out: the slow subtracting depths
Rose up; boldly he chinned the ruffling wave,
And wide the lifting side-cloths flowed, and fast
He mowed the watery swathes. She idly sat
Watching his knife-like knees divide and slide,
Slide and divide: only the hissing silks
Susurrous foamed about her.
Far from mainland and manland they swam,
Past many an island shawled and shimmering
In haze. The antlered trees stood still to gaze
At the amazing sight. On the shores
A thousand doors opened needle eyes
To take their thready beauty.
And O the mowers marching in the meadows,
And O the lowing cows. Still they swam on
Into the silent noon and ambience

Of sea so vast they hardly seemed to move
On its grave glass: its same and lazy glaze
Moored them everywhere. Still her eyes
Slid in their slotted cells, and still she searched
The satchels under her. There in a green night
The cloudy fish sailed by, too thin
To have a shadow, too light to have a stay.
And there were wandering veils that bellied up
And ebbed like blushes. Thready shapes of breath
Mouthed once, and went unsaid as innuendos
Under the stones. And O the blowing glooms
And overtones, the many streams that bore
From floor to floor the shining minnow-shoals
In rainbow rows that tore the smoky mane
With fire. Dug upon dug, tug upon tug
Of beauty fed Europa, till at last
She clapped her eyes and sang —

In what melodious mould
Was first this body rolled,
How was it overwashed
By winds, what rainbows lashed
Its eyes, what musics conched its ears,
What cataracts it broke
And tore to tags and smoke
That slowly wore it round and smooth as weirs,
And woods, too, grew in it, and volleys
Of finches flashed in all its valleys.
Only in soil the soul
Grows, and is coarsely whole,
For spirit has its commonplace and base;
Four seas conferred to build,
Four seasons too fulfilled
This body's scope, and gave it meaning and grace

Till from its bottle-loins there sprang
A hissing head and rocket-fang
Of life whose spittle drooped and spread
Its silver drivellings overhead,
Breaking the cold and middle ceiling,
And heavens hymeneal and farther-off revealing.

. . . . .

Midway they met
Where daylight and delight broke through the roof.
There in a tambourine clearing of shaking leaves,
Where nightly the ambient moth on its undulate thong
Of nothingness dances, she flashed;
She at the touch of whose name
All his tongue's tapers would flame.
O what wonders can happen in woods
Or in words, what two may touch, what gloom
Can ignite, halves hyphenate; what dead ends
And ands join answering hands.
As when the rounding sounding bee at last
Alights and kisses the sill of its stillness,
Its singing skein at length wound into a ball,
So all his dreamy wanderings had come
To one true pass; here through the gate of horn
They threaded to be born. Why should she shir
And shudder then? Scared by his lashing air
She curled back into gloom,
The silent pleas of her eyes
Jumping from place to place
Of his bold unblinking stare. Cold, he thought,
Cold as cut-glass
That holds a burning eye of candle-light
Her body is. Its beauty's to distract

The tender lover, its answer's to deflect
His anxious longing and to make it linger
In thinking ways; it fractures and delays
His single gaze. That hovering face,
That cold shoulder and the swelling hopes
Below, have no warm arm or base
To widen or embrace one.
But stiff, as if in alarm,
She bristles into beauty. O a thousand thistles
Of glass and kisses of ice she is.
Fire in a thousand mirrors is the eye
That looks at her with warmth; and each light facet shows
Only a dancing midge, a jigging image
Of changing joy. Gently on the swell
Of her he rose and fell, reflectively.
Then as between two lifts the candle-flame
Sinks to rise stiff, tip-toe, and finger-still,
Stretching at length to its ecstatic aim
As if from slackness it had drawn its fill,
So on knees of night the bull sank
Lowly to his socket,
And so — all stitches stretched — on toes of light
The god rose slowly. How could she not,
Hooked-up to that hawkpoint of hovering love,
Feel fear? Seeing him assume
That luminous image, did she divine
The blind millennium of mind behind
The upstart moment, the deep duplicity
Of flesh and spirit, clod and cloud, the make-and-break
Of clamouring animal and calm god,
And man the amalgam?
Ah but she had neither ear nor air
For argument, who now could only stare,
Round, thoughtless, oughtless, at the shapeless god,

Who slowly rose before her.
In tiers and terraces went clambering up,
Out of his huff of hooves, his blazing cape
And carapace of darkness, covering all
The clinging undertow of dearth like hope.
And in that darkness wrestled the lone god,
Jolted in every joint like elbowing flame
That strove for overthrow. What here had grasp
Of anything? What smoke-scream called him forth
So suddenly? She saw his osier-arms
Sprout, his fisted hooves fray into finger-fronds,
The abrupt bull-neck extenuate. A shin
Inched up to knee and sunshined into thigh.
Back into lack the entrances all led,
But all the vents evoked the forward god
Who rose and faced Europa.

. . . . .

Here on the sill
Of silence and assent
She waited wordless, though her body spoke.
As trundling thunders pause
And pitch their lightning tents upon the hush,
Or as the darkling bird
Crowds all its longings into one last rush, so
Her backward breasts like trumped-up charges rose
And brazened out his coming. Three times
Three times the dust thrilled and throbbed
And rills of answer ran between the stones.
Three times the rod gulped and pulsed
Like shaken rope.
And louder drummed the blood-light in his ears,
Stiffer the lift, rounder the hour at last

That struck for home. Love, like a lick of oil,
That softly clicks the lock and often,
Slid over her then and loosed her backward wards
To one sprung cry — 'Zeus!' O the fountain-throw!
The twitching hitch! the quiet!

Go, sun and moon! Come, musk and cinnamon,
Assume me now;
Sing me the dying god, the night's denial and
The light cock-crow.
Let all the mournful musics flow
Over his morning deeps, and mask
The blind bull bellowing slow, the sea-bell
Tolling low in funeral-gloom.
Light fails within the wood.
The last, the best pieces of brightness fall
Into the base grasses that appropriate all.
O, as grass amasses grass,
May sleep after sleep, loved over by leaves,
Engross those two, house them and hush them
In arms of amaranth,
And may the nodding moth of myth
In every mouth take breath and wing now,
And dance these words out in honour of that wedding.

The Fall

O angel of the ledges of our dread
On whose jellied edges each joy is dandled
Gently, like danger — now, like daws on trees
Unbalancing, turn our dread into ease
And let the fall open our wings' eyes wide
In wonder at ourselves who were so slow
To float out on the rootless raft of air
With flowing hold.
The Fall! the fall, from that safe tree
Of love we so much feared to leave, elates
And lifts our other selves to life. Only
By daring do we learn our manyness.
Safety stints us, turns us to stone, to one.
This always-gibbering between fear and hope
Doubles our life, and is the bloody pulse
Of every vein. O angel of our dread,
Delicately cater for us rough feeders
Who ask a stone; and duly give us bread.

The Trinity

Down the darkened hall of brain
Darts the tiny mouse of pain,
Quick as thought the waking cat
Of consciousness scoots from the mat,

Elastically catches it,
Statically lets it go
Slack again, but snatches it
Lightly back on its yo-yo.

Till in the vast and breathing hall
A thousand sleepers wake and call
'Curse the cat and curse the mouse,
— And curse, God curse, this bloody house'.

God who did send this I to cry
Between two selves on Calvary,
God who in darkness all forlorn
Between two thieving moods was torn,

(The nagging cat of thought, the mouse
Of niggling guilt that runs this house)
Make these two malefactors one
Within this I
That soon must die,
And then will rise the Sun, the Sun,
The trinity, the three-in-one.

Nativity

His holly hair, his berry eyes are here,
And his chrysanthemum wound,
This Christmas day; by symbols once again
The Mystery's importuned.

Hisses the singing kettle of his blood
Out of his sanguine side,
Poked by the sibling spear it ebbs and flows
In a hub-bubble tide

That dyes the silent room. The gay young god,
Dog in the manger now,
Growls in the hearth, and bares old teeth against
The Ass in us, the Cow.

There are the portly bottle-loins, and there
The wine-marks of his birth
Upon the straw, the biscuit-brittle straw
Broken by Mary's girth.

And here, most meek, most eager and most hushed,
The angelic agents hover,
A great prudential company, all come
To offer him life-cover.

Comes sentiment with frozen tears lent
By memory, melting sweet,
Her hothead cries boil over and congeal
Again at her cold feet.

And Grief, deep in her crushed and tinfoil wrap,
Brokenly glares today
Among the ashes and the cruel butt-
Ends of this Christmas play.

And there's the tapering tree of his descent,
Hitched to a kingly star,
Earth is its horizontal, heaven and hell
Its upright centre-spar.

The very tree of life, so base, so wide,
And with such longing fraught,
Up the step-ladder of our looks it spires
Into a point of thought.

In the stark winter of our tinselled pride
Its frozen growth now stands
Waiting the fiery gift, the melting dew
Spangled from heavenly hands.

Ah look! the bush is candleabraed now
With yellow and with blue,
Types of the spirit, sweet and bitter both,
Opposed but wholly true.

Outside, like rootless souls the silent trees
Sail past on trays of mist;
The miser-icicle on the pane still marks
The place that Judas kissed.

His thistle breath still lingers in the air,
Spiky with eagerness,
It hovers on the garden, and the grass
Whitens at his caress.

Robin with rusty bib no longer can
Pull out the worm-like nail,
Dumpy with impotence it droops and humps
Upon the wooden rail.

And hark! the Herod-angels sing to-night!
Over the Magi's tents
Their heartless song drones on through grumbling glooms
And weeping continents.

High on his farthing floor the airman moons
Above the mourning town
Of Bethlehem; it is his fiddling root
And he the flower and crown.

O Caspar, Melchior, and Balthazar,
Come from your caravan
And tell me where you go, and what new star
You saw in Teheran:

And what new man now hurries to be born
Out of our addled earth,
And O what silly corner of ourselves
Will see the mangy birth.

Strike, strike the gong of our song till souls take fire,
Clap hands and bellow,
Dance, dance, leap higher and longer, and hug
Each with its fellow.

Lord, in this wintry interval we send
Our indolent regards
And grey regrets. Make fluent all the pens
Of all the frozen bards.

Lay the live coal upon their lips that they
May leap uproariously
Out of their huff of words, and let the thorns
Crackle with prophecy.

Resume, and reimburse the silent wood,
Elaborate its saps,
Bid the bare trees blurt into bloom, and fill
With leaf the hungry gaps,
And in its head set the heart's singing birds.

Carol

Deep in the fading leaves of night
There lay the flower that darkness knows,
Till winter stripped and brought to light
The most incomparable Rose
That blows, that blows.

The flashing mirrors of the snow
Keep turning and returning still:
To see the lovely child below
And hold him is their only will;
Keep still, keep still.

And to let go his very cry
The clinging echoes are so slow
That still his wail they multiply
Though he lie singing now below,
So low, so low.

Even the doves forget to grieve
And gravely to his greeting fly
And the lone places that they leave
All follow and are standing by
On high, on high.

The Journey of the Magi

Behold there came wise men from the east, saying, Where is he,
  for we have seen his star?

It was a dark January night, cold and snowing
When the Three Kings started out
On their annual journey: and what on earth
They were doing — and such a time to be going!
And, honestly, what it was all about
Not one of them knew. But they wanted a birth,
A new lift, as we all do. Was the journey wise? —
Yes, or No? Well, that was anybody's guess
As it still is: a risk. A different address
May only land you in a different kind of a mess.
Put it no higher than that. But still, there was the Star
Throbbing in front like a bell, bobbing them on from afar,
Regardless of hail, rain, or snow, or glitter or glar.
The Three Kings marched away into the west,
To one dark enterprise they were addressed.
There was nowhere they would not go, feast or fast,
Slum or salon, bethel or brothel, if only at last
And at least they could come to the truth and be blessed.
Perhaps in some far corner of the world
An answer lay, a sleeping past was curled.
February now, the driving swathes of rain
Swaddle the hills that edge the Atlantic main,
And wave on wave like superimposing hands
Slip and withdraw on Europe's farthest strands.
Through the wet night the Three Kings rode away,
It mattered not who called on them to stay:
It matters not who dances or who sings
They must away to find the King of Kings.

To welcome gravity, and to forego fun
Is still their fate who seek the heavenly One
And choose the Star.

And now the month is March,
Bloodbursty buds are pink upon the larch.
One thing about journeys which is rather good
— Things never happen how and where they should,
God, for example, as the Three Kings found,
Is seldom above-board, but underground;
And on the other hand, the Devil
Is to be met on almost every level,
High place and holy day. The guide-book's Star
Has small relation to things as they are.
Still, one lives and learns that saints, if fat,
Are none the earthier or the worse for that;
God can be sought for in a golden rain
Of levity and fireworks; piety's not pain.
The guns go off, the rockets fly
Over the Kings now riding by.
In passing, one may duly note
That reverence need not choke the throat
Or dull the cheek.
It's only those
Who hug the sober truth, the gloomy ones,
Who always fear to let off their guns.
Truth's never sober, but, like a wayward gipsy
She wears the loudest colours, shouts, and goes half-tipsy.
Now up, now down, now gay, now melancholy,
Now drawn to hope and now pursued by folly,
The Three Kings marched zigzag, a star their brolly.
Caspar got blind one night, Melchior met a lady,
Balthazar was involved in something shady;
Strange that, in lands, and countries quite unknown,

We find, not others' strangeness, but our own;
That is one use of journeys; if one delves,
Differently, one's sure to find one's selves.
O in what wildernesses of one another
We wander looking for ourselves! What bother
We go through, what cold, what heat
To find the answer up our own back street.
Meanwhile this gipsy life the Three Kings led, as unconfined
As the May bloom that blithely takes the wind.
A man comes up to the Three Kings and cries
'I'm an insurance agent; I advise —
In case you're tempted, sirs, to trust your eyes —
Take out a policy, against surprise.
Seeing's believing; journeys are dangerous things;
Belief can lay its icy hand on Kings.
For a small premium we will give relief
In case of sickness, second sight, belief;
But if at sixty-five you're still quite blind,
You'll get a bonus; our company's that kind.
Just answer these few questions: — Have you had
Father or Mother who was ill or mad
Or bad enough to see things as they are?
Did any of your family see a star?
Barring that — ' With that they pushed the man away;
Live dangerously, see all, and come what may,
Was their belief.
The Three Kings hitched their wagon to the Star
And gave the Star its head. Now near, now far,
Now in, now out, now to and fro it led;
Never straight. Journeys are always curly,
Like comets or like hairpins they are meant
To crown or to lead up to some event.
Herod did all he could do to prevent
Their coming. This journey had its hazards.

He broke the poles, and he cut the wires,
He stole their pump and deflated their tyres,
And he turned their messengers into liars;
But in vain.
He muffled the knocker, disconnected the bell,
Turned up his radio till it howled like hell,
Changed his name and address as well;
But in vain.

After October with its fiery leaf
Came grey November, frozen, as in grief;
Dumpy with impotence King Herod sat,
Not even bothering to take off his hat,
When in came the Three Kings, as if by chance,
And Herod rose and made great song and dance
About them. Black Caspar said to Balthazar
'He's a good sort, Herod; there's no colour-bar
With him.' 'May be,' said Melchior, 'but why
Does he keep staring up into the sky?
And why's he quizzing us about the Star?'
'O just some complex,' Caspar said, 'to do with power:
Rank has its obligations, and in fact
The first is to preserve itself intact.'
— So they argued on, intent;
Till suddenly, above the Palace towers
They saw their guiding star turn red, like Mars,
And knew that it was angry. Bloody wars
It threatened. And at once they went
Without good-byes.

December now; the Three Kings stood
Benighted in the deepest wood,
The wits-end of their hardihood.
No longer kings, but helpless now

They threw away their golden bough;
They stamped upon their golden crowns
And damned the country, damned the towns.
They'd lost the Star, their only link
And anchor-light. O not a blink
No hope, no help in earth or sky!
— They gave a last despairing cry.
Then suddenly all raised a shout
For overhead the Star flared out
Just like a fan: and there they saw
In the last ditch, on the last straw,
In front of them a heavenly child.
See! it looked up at them and smiled.
It was the child within themselves
For which they'd sought, for which Age delves
— Now Age and Innocence can meet,
Now, now the circle is complete,
The journey's done. Lord, Lord, how sweet!

Christ Walking on the Water

Slowly, O so slowly, longing rose up
In the forenoon of his face, till only
A ringlet of fog lingered round his loins.
And fast he went down beaches all weeping
With weed, and waded out. Twelve tall waves,
Sequent and equated, hollowed and followed.
O what a cock-eyed sea he walked on,
What poke-ends of foam, what elbowings
And lugubrious looks, what ebullient
And contumacious musics. Always there were
Hills and holes, pills and poles, a wavy wall
And bucking ribbon caterpillaring past
With glossy ease. And often, as he walked,
The slow curtains of swell swung open and showed,
Miles and smiles away, the bottle-boat
Flung on a wavering frond of froth that fell
Knee-deep and heaved thigh-high. In his forward face
No cave of afterthought opened; to his ear
No bottom clamour climbed up; nothing blinked.
For he was the horizon, he the hub,
Both bone and flesh, finger and ring of all
This clangourous sea. Docile, at his toe's touch
Each tottering dot stood roundaboutly calm
And jammed the following others fast as stone.
The ironical wave smoothed itself out
To meet him, and the mocking hollow
Hooped its back for his feet. A spine of light
Sniggered on the knobbly water, ahead.
But he like a lover, caught up,
Pushed past all wrigglings and remonstrances

And entered the rolling belly of the boat
That shuddered and lay still. And he lay there
Emptied of his errand, oozing still. Slowly
The misted mirror of his eyes grew clear
And cold, the bell of blood tolled lower,
And bright before his sight the ocean bared
And rolled its horrible bold eye-balls endlessly
In round rebuke. Looking over the edge
He shivered. Was this the way he had come?
Was that the one who came? The whole wieldy world
And all the welded welt that he had walked on
Burst like a plate into purposelessness.
All, all was gone, the fervour and the froth
Of confidence, and flat as water was
The sad and glassy round. Somewhere, then,
A tiny flute wriggled like a worm, O so lonely.
A ring of birds rose up and wound away
Into nothingness. Beyond himself he saw
The settled steeples, and breathing beaches
Running with people. But he,
He was custodian to nothing now,
And boneless as an empty sleeve hung down.
Down from crowned noon to cambered evening
He fell, fell, from white to amber, till night
Slid over him like an eyelid. And he,
His knees drawn up, his head dropped deep,
Curled like a question mark asleep.

Resurrection

An Easter Sequence

> '*O vos omnes,*
> *Qui transitis per viam, et videte,*
> *Si est dolor similis sicut dolor meus,*
> *Attendite universi populi, et videte*
> *dolorem meum, dolorem meum.*'

Tell ye the daughter of Sion, Behold thy King cometh unto thee . . .

It was a deliberate moment, and O
Just in the nick and nook of time he came,
The timeless One, to reclaim us. Everything waited,
Everything peaked and pointed to his coming.
The morning rose up early, a tip toe of a day,
All was light and elastic, the birds chirping away,
The air chipped into buds. People were on their knees
With wonder, and some were weeping. And when at last He
    appeared
—The Hero—such a hail of huzzas and hosannahs as sprang
    up!
Why, the very house-tops rose to the occasion and broke
Their hush and hung out all their hearts' hoorays.
This was glory. Yet, he knew the swings of men, and now
It was the old story.
The day too bright to last, the crowd too loud to stay.
Those who magnified now would mock Him tomorrow,
Those who deified, defy. Already He saw
The shadow of Doubt, that pickpocket of conviction,
Move through the crowd. And far away and behind
Their fume and furore of glory he heard the door
Of doom slam; meanwhile all was gay
And like a King he came triumphant up this way.

And when He was come into Jerusalem, all the city was moved, saying,
   Who is this?

O it was no day at all for doubt or for cloud,
The children ran cheering in front, the birds sang loud,
The very trees were bowed; and the butterfly leaves
Took off to greet him.
But he rode loftily by as if uninvolved in the glory,
And the ass, as if understanding the story,
Carried him sadly on to a tame
And lamentable conclusion.
To meet with all and go with none
That was his doom who mediates and makes one
The split that was in man since time began.
But how to heal the breach? how to reach across?
Ay, that was the only answer now — the Cross!
Deep in his mind the roots ran that way, and his fate
Was fixed. The tree was grown that stood on Calvary,
What was to do was done. Still, it was a glad day.
Let the bells all ring, let them have their fling,
For this way led to glory and to everlasting Spring.

Now when the even was come, he sat down with the twelve.

> Twelve heads hugged in a ring
> Twelve hands breaking bread
> Twelve hearts bursting to sing
> The song of life from the dead.

Now the moment had come; he must love them and leave them
Yet without losing; this is the mystery of losing.
In the world, of course, it is different; there, every love of life
Of person, place, or thing, is a boon and a beauty

That comes in the morning so freely. Yet, in the afternoon,
Fearful of losing it we freeze it into a duty
And judge it our due. And then what surprise
When in the evening it dies.
O if only we had faith enough not to confine
And coffin the thing that we love, faith enough to receive
It just when it came, insight enough to let go and believe
That each morning would bring it again,
We would not have to grieve over the thing that was slain.
So he spoke to them at supper, so he figured it forth
In the breaking of bread
To those who were his twelve selves, dear as his own soul.
For all these selves his soul had for sieves
To let fall his story
As snow falls in flakes; yet who knows if it gives
One half of what it knows of the whole glory.

*And as they did eat, he said, Verily I say unto you, that one of you shall
betray me.*

Name him not, Name him not, nor constellate
The one who led him to his fate. Nevertheless
Judas was part of Jesus.
For the god has always a foot of clay, and the soul
Grows in soil, the flower has a dark root.
And deep in all is the base collaborator.
The betrayer is ever oneself, never another.
All must say, 'Lord is it I?' There is always
Evil in Goodness, lust in love, dust on the dove's foot,
And without it purity's groundless. And the Cross
Had never been.

Then cometh Jesus with them unto a place called Gethsemane.

It was a lovely night,
A night for weddings and for water.
Going out into the cold glow he felt washed
And clean of people. The garden had an air
Of waiting about it, as if the leaves were bent
On eavesdropping. And the rain
Scented the air with more-than-midnight pain.
And the wet trees that had nowhere to go
Stood round and gazed at the One walking there below
In agony. Ebb and flow, to and fro, Yes and No;
Doubt assailed him. Which and what to do? This much must be
    admitted,
We live between two worlds, faith and doubt,
Like breath. The air that one breathes does not care
Whether it's in or out; it's not in love with life
Or death. And yet we do not dare to hold it long,
But must let go to find again. So with faith,
With love, with everything. Now at the cross-roads,
Middled and muddled he stood.
This was it. And it was night. 'Nevertheless Thy will be done.'
That thought made morning of it, gave him ease, and issue.
He knew now how to stay and stare it out
And already the torches approached the garden.

Now Peter sat without in the palace.

Tenebrae now; and quenched as if by doubt
One after one the torches all go out
In token of the twelve who went away
Each after other on the fatal day.
That fateful night,

Late in the palace, something strange occured.
A spider lit on his hand, and he threw it away
But it returned to his hand on a thread;
He threw it away again, and again away,
And again till his fingers were dripping
And webbed with threads, but, horrible! still it **came back**
Like a truth that could not be denied,
The truth he had three times denied;
Peter desisted. He listened. In the cold dawn
The cock was throwing aloft its threefold crown
And aureole of sound. Then he remembered
The meaning.
In the dark blue and petering hour
Of night it sang, and looking out,
He saw the tree dance into flower
Enlisting all the morning's light;
It was the bloody Judas tree,
And on it hung not him, but *me*.

Whether of the twain will ye that I release unto you? **They said, Barabbas.**

We will always beg the question.
Jesus did not belong to this time;
Their clocks all said he came before his chime,
All the lamps of the city declared him a stranger,
A nobody come out of darkness, and therefore **a danger**
To law and to order. Must it always be so?
Must we always make light of the devil we **know**
And dark of the god who is ranger? O
It is easy to choose what's dead right, right
— So we say — to refuse to live wrong; so we **move**
In thick circles of self, and the lean dog-rose
Looks for the hole in our hedge and lurks

In our thorn waiting to leap out of lack
Into bloom like the god in the manger.

And when he had scourged Jesus, he delivered him to be crucified.

They took him out to die.
The lark was shaking out its acres of song in the sky
And the sun shone. People looked up and remarked
What a wonderful day it was going to be
And the cheering boys ran on in front of the crowd,
And the cheeky ones waited to stare.
                              Once he noticed
A blind man whom he had healed looking at him
With horrified eyes as much as to say
'Was it for this I was given sight by the god that day?'
He turned away. If only this had been an important death,
If only he knew that the people who barracked him now
Had been travelling years and years to reach this place.
But they were casual passers-by and their interest was jaded.
Yet it was all as he had expected, and
He would not avoid or evade it. Far away
A spool of birds was spinning above the hill,
And still Pilate sat in the empty court beneath,
Sucking threads of thoughtfulness through his teeth.

And they crucified him.

This was a rough death, there was nothing tidy about it,
No sweetness, nothing noble.
Everything stuck out awkwardly and angular:
The clumsy soldier brought the wrong basket of nails;
And the couriers — those sticky fly-papers of events —

Did not even bother to cover his sticky end,
Or carry it home to Rome. For them the war in Gaul
Was more important; the ship of state sailed on,
Leaving him bogging in the backward seas.
Still, that is how things always happen, lousily,
But later on, the heart edits them lovingly,
Abstracts the jeers and jags, imports a plan
Into the pain, and calls it history.
We always go back to gloss over some roughness,
To make the past happen properly as we want it to happen.
But this was a hard death. At the time
There was no room for thought.
How often he had hearsed and rehearsed this hour.
But when you come up against it all the good words about it
Are less than breath. It is hard to turn the other cheek
When both have been slapped:
                              Yes, it was a hard death.

Now there stood by the Cross of Jesus his mother . . .

A mist opened and closed its eyes before him,
And in it he saw her looking at him
The untouchable terrible god.
O what ladders of longing led up from her
To him, what steps and depths of memory ran down;
He remembered the happy days in Galilee
When he was heaven's hub; the heap of smoking grass,
The bubble-pipe, the light upon the wall,
The children in the far garden looking for the lost ball,
And Mary calling him. He was always so distant
In those lonely days. O if only
He had mattered less, she wondered, if only
She had mastered him more, would he then

Have been like other men, a flat satisfied plain?
But no. In him mountains of onlyness rose
Snow-high. Dayspring was in his eyes
At midnight. And he would not come down
From his far purpose even for her who was
The root that raised him to this Cross and crown
Of thorns. Yet tenderly he spoke
Good-bye now, his voice choking and dry.
And as she went away, leaving him to die,
The vast moon of his cry rose up upon the darkness.
His heart broke.

About the ninth hour Jesus cried with a loud voice, saying, Eli, Eli,
   lama sabacthani?

His breath came in threads; his words were not his own.
He was dying now.
The sun refused to look, and the sky
Closed up its eye. Only the windows of his wounds
Were wide open, and the red curtains of blood
Blew out into the storm, torn to ribbons.
He could no longer fend death off.
Slow, slow, loath to go, hope holds up its head
Though feet are so sawn through, like a sawn tree that stands
Long, then with one blinding run and blundering tear
Of last despair, scattering its brains and branches on the air
Slumps, lumps, pitches headlong and thuds, a log clodded clean.
So his last cry and acquiescence. And the vast wall
Of people drew back before that dying fall.
God was dead.

And, behold, the veil of the temple was rent in twain from the top to the
  bottom; and the earth did quake and the rocks rent;

Now was the world's back broken; the darkness
Heaved in half, the wells rose up in walls
And fell in floods; and earth's own gorge
Rose and retched out its coffins. Everywhere
Lightnings lashed, and the curled thunder rolled
Its bolts over the crowd that broke and ran before its crash.
Each flash showed them in a different flight.
And in the downpour only the soldiers stood
Sodden and awed beneath the Cross. 'This was the son of God!'
To them the eliminating moment was
The illuminating one. Now all was still.
And on the desolate plain behind the hill
An ass brayed. Its palmy days were over.

And there was Mary Magdalene and the other Mary, sitting over against
  the sepulchre . . .

It is always the women who are the Watchers
And keepers of life: they guard our exits
And our entrances. They are both tomb and womb,
End and beginning. Bitterly they bring forth
And bitterly take back the light they gave.
The last to leave and still the first to come,
They circle us like sleep or like the grave.
Earth is their element, and in it lies
The seed and silence of the lighted skies,
The seasons with their fall and slow uprise,
Man with his sight and militant surmise.
It is always the women who are the Watchers
And Wakeners.

In the end of the Sabbath, as it began to dawn toward the first day of
   the week, came Mary Magdalene.

The tomb, the tomb, that
Was her core and care, her one sore.
The light had hardly scarleted the dark
Or the first bird sung when Mary came in sight
With eager feet. Grief, like last night's frost,
Whitened her face and tightened all her tears.
It was there, then, there at the blinding turn
Of the bare future that she met her past.
She only heard his Angel tell her how
The holding stone broke open and gave birth
To her dear Lord, and how his shadow ran
To meet him like a dog.
And as the sun
Burns through the simmering muslins of the mist
Slowly his darkened voice, that seemed like doubt,
Morninged into noon; the summering bees
Mounted and boiled over in the bell-flowers.
'Come out of your jail, Mary,' he said, 'the doors are open
And joy has its ears cocked for your coming.
Earth now is no place to mope in. So throw away
Your doubt, cast every clout of care,
Hang all your hallelujahs out
This airy day.'

Lent

Mary Magdalene, that easy woman,
Saw, from the shore, the seas
Beat against the hard stone of Lent,
Crying, 'Weep, seas, weep
For yourselves that cannot dent me more.

O more than all these, more crabbed than all stones,
And cold, make me, who once
Could leap like water, Lord. Take me
As one who owes
Nothing to what she was. Ah, naked.

My waves of scent, my petticoats of foam
Put from me and rebut;
Disown. And that salt lust stave off
That slavered me — O
Let it whiten in grief against the stones

And outer reefs of me. Utterly doff,
Nor leave the lightest veil
Of feeling to heave or soften.
Nothing cares this heart
What hardness crates it now or coffins.

Over the balconies of these curved breasts
I'll no more peep to see
The light procession of my loves
Surf-riding in to me
Who now have eyes and alcove, Lord, for Thee.'

'Room, Mary,' said He, 'ah make room for me
Who am come so cold now
To my tomb.' So, on Good Friday,
Under a frosty moon
They carried Him and laid Him in her womb.

A grave and icy mask her heart wore twice,
But on the third day it thawed,
And only a stone's-flow away
Mary saw her God.
Did you hear me? Mary saw her God!

Dance, Mary Magdalene, dance, dance and sing,
For unto you is born
This day a King. 'Lady,' said He,
'To you who relent
I bring back the petticoat and the bottle of scent.'

The Net

Quick, woman, in your net
Catch the silver I fling!
O I am deep in your debt,
Draw tight, skin-tight, the string,
And rake the silver in.
No fisher ever yet
Drew such a cunning ring.

Ah, shifty as the fin
Of any fish this flesh
That, shaken to the shin,
Now shoals into your mesh,
Bursting to be held in;
Purse-proud and pebble-hard,
Its pence like shingle showered.

Open the haul, and shake
The fill of shillings free,
Let all the satchels break
And leap about the knee
In shoals of ecstasy.
Guineas and gills will flake
At each gull-plunge of me.

Though all the Angels, and
Saint Michael at their head,
Nightly contrive to stand
On guard about your bed,
Yet none dare take a hand,

But each can only spread
His eagle-eye instead.

But I, being man, can kiss
And bed-spread-eagle too;
All flesh shall come to this,
Being less than angel is,
Yet higher far in bliss
As it entwines with you.

Come, make no sound, my sweet;
Turn down the candid lamp
And draw the equal quilt
Over our naked guilt.

Stormy Night

Is this the street? Never a sign of life,
The swinging lamp throws everything about;
But see! from that sly doorway, like a knife
The gilt edge of inviting light slides out
And in again — the very sign
Of her whose slightest nod I lately thought was mine;

But not now.
Knock! and the night-flowering lady
Opens, and across the brilliant sill
Sees me standing there so dark and shady
Hugging the silences of my ill-will;
Wildly she turns from me — But no, my love,
This foot's within the door, this hand's without the glove.

Well may you tremble now, and say there was nothing meant,
And curl away from my care with a 'Please, my dear!',
For though you were smoke, sucked up by a raging vent,
I'd follow you through every flue of your fear,
And over your faraway arms I'll mountain and cone
In a pillar of carolling fire and fountaining stone.

O strike the gong of your wrong, raise the roof of your rage
Fist and foist me off with a cloud of cries,
What do I care for all your footling rampage?
On your light-in-gale blows my larking caresses will rise,
But — Why so still? What! are you weeping, my sweet?
Ah heart, heart, look! I throw myself at your feet.

The Harvest Field

There is nothing to note; only the mowers
Moving like doom. Slowly, one by one,
A gloom of bees rises and soon snores
Thunder-headed away into the sun.

Listen! Listen! Do you hear the hiss
Of the scythe in the long grasses
That are silently tingling like bells that kiss
And repel as the wind passes?

There in the last care and core of corn
The hare is couched: not till the mowers flash
Their smiling scythes, and all its walls are shorn
Will the wild creatures dash
Into the wintry air of hound and horn.

Listen! Listen! Do you hear the hiss
Of the scythe in the long grasses of your laughter?
More is mowed than you know, for this
Is Time's swathe, and you are the one that he's after.

The Swan

Bottomed by tugging combs of water
The slow and loath swan slews and looks
Coldly down through chutes of stilled chatter
Upon the shadows in flight among the stones.

Into abashed confusions of ooze
It dips, and from the muddy fume
The silver and flute-like fishes rise
Endlessly up through all their octaves of gloom

To where the roofed swan suavely swings
Without qualm on the quivering wave
That laves it on, with elbowing wings held wide
Under its eyes' hugged look and architrave.

Jonquil-long its neck adjudicates
Its body's course; aloof and cool
It cons the nonchalant and unseeing air
With its incurious and dispassionate stare.

Slow, slow, it slides, as if not to chafe
The even sleeve of its approach
Stretched stiff and oval in front of it,
Siphoning it on, selfless, silent, and safe.

On that grey lake, frilled round with scufflings
Of foam and milled with muttering,
I saw lingering, late and lightless,
A single swan, swinging, sleek as a sequin.

Negligently bright, wide wings pinned back,
It mooned on the moving water,
And not all the close and gartering dark
Or gathering wind could lift or flatter

That small and dimming image into flight;
Far from shore and free from foresight,
Coiled in its own indifferent mood
It held the heavens, shores, waters and all their brood.

Spring

From my wind-blown book I look
Up and see the lazy rook
Rise and twist away,
And from every airy eave
The arrowy swallows wildly leave
And swoop as if in play.

Dark the daw with claw-wing sail
Swings at anchor in the gale,
And in the running grass
Daffodils nod and intervene
Like sud-flecks on a sea of green
Dissolving as they pass.

Mouldy and old the bouldered walls
Wake in the sun and warm their polls
And wag aubretia beards,
The snail-gaze of senility
Silvers each front, and backward they
Break wind and dree their weirds.

Bosoms of bloom that sob like moss
Beneath each jumpy breath, emboss
The bony orchard's breast;
And look, the leggy lilac canes
Are varicosed with ivy veins
Of envy coalesced.

There the hare, bound after bound,
Concertinas all the ground
As far as eye can spy it,
Like a fountain's dying spray
It falls in little frills away
Into a twitching quiet.

Still down the slow opposing slope
The intent ploughman draws his rope
Of parsimony fine,
Nor sees bold Icarus in his haste
Expend his spirit in a waste
Of aerobatic wine.

Icarus from his heady plane
Into depths of spinning brain
Bales out like a ball,
Pulls the ripcord, splits the sack
And lets the spilled silk splutter back
And speculative fall.

And hark, the lark sarcastic sings
To Icarus without his wings
Dawdling down the sky,
Indolent aeons have gone to make
Its gimlet bill, its song-gill's shake,
Its all-containing cry.

Spring-Dance

Late, late. But lift now the diffident fiddle and fill
The dancing bed with light and the bud-room with thunder
Till all the floors fall in and walls laugh under
The envious knockings of neighbours, and over the sill
The daffodil day looks in. You who are standing,
Yes you — kick up your kilt of legs like a gawky foal
And fling away there! On every leaf-landing
The lovers are forking, on every stair-air
They are larking: the dog-days are barking
In all the backyards. So off with your careful sark
And lift the diffident fiddle. O the lilt's not difficult, if
You have soil in your soul. God in the clod, then, begin
And cloud into powder your foot and fetlock of clay
As you clout the floor and claw your next-of-skin
In a fug of guffaws. Ah, there's never a fog
That fails to ivy and over the wall of its huff
And hangover. Not even a gruff one who won't
Give a heave — and a fig for all leaves! — and have after,
(How the daft words proliferate in me like laughter!)
As Jack after Jill. So off with your careful sark and lift
The diffident fiddle. Can no one cajole you
To hyphenate hands in the dance, and piece out its pauses
With passes? Listen! The night-cocks are throwing their
    crowing
Far beyond sight of their own height and knowing
Into the light. You, only, are lacking
The jocular glow. Look how the gales brag and bring
Surprises of birds all paradised-over by Spring.

Summer Journey

Now it's July, hot and sleepy and still;
The noontide hanging motionless over the hill
Like a pike in a pool. And the glossy flies
Are flashing like great sun-whips across the eyes.
Summer is at its height,
The hastening season halted in its flight,
Its fans fixed.
And here we are in the Pays-Basque, travelling through Soule,
Labourd, and Basse-Navarre — names more musical to me
Than musk or kumiss or mangosteen.
Guéthary where the Atlantic curled in and cauliflowered up,
And the lightning jagged the sky like icicles:
Bidarry in the evening, the vines veining the hillside,
And the hills drawn up over our heads like shawls.
And us talking all night of war and Resistance.
Remember the Pyrenees, with their hundred double-chins,
Remember Soure, the sheep bells on the road,
And the panniered donkeys; the smuggler's path to Spain,
And the lovely inns; the meal at Mauléon;
The mayor's home-made liquor at Ustaritz
That Sunday afternoon. O
Remember the people so kind: remember the night you got blind
On Pernod?
And remember those great sleepy houses with their wide and
    wavy roofs
That cover cattle and people and wine and copper pans:
Houses eyelashed and shuttered against the summer heat,
Blindly white outside but with nests of darkness in them
As reticent and withdrawn as the Basques with their
    thin-pursed lips.

Slow country, rooted in resistance, not in rest.
Slow over the wall the fat peaches fall.
Slowly across the all-absorbing fields
Collusive move the peasant and his plough.
And slowly down the street the ox comes now
With winking bell. How it gives one the feel
Of the creaking cart and the ever-turning wheel.
Slow country, but quick people. What's so gay
As the little Basque drum tipping and tapping away
To the agile pipe that wriggles about like an eel.
Remember the group who sang in the café that day?
And the village fête on Sunday where we saw
The circle of life complete, saw the day
Turn from morning to night, from light to grey,
And the people counterwise from grave to gay,
From church to dance and then from dance to play.
Sunday morning, seven by the clock,
And the village silent except for the cock
Ricochetting far away: and over the roof
Are the dark Pyrenees, overweening and aloof
As ever. A boy comes into the square
And a pigeon rises and flashes the rosy air.
Never was morning so clear. And one by one
A rope of bees bubbles up into the sun.
A bell is calling the people to early Mass,
The doors open, I watch the church-goers pass
To where within the ancient womb
A blaze of incense and a bloom
Of candles ring the bridegroom-priest
Who bodies forth the Mystery
That has been all men's history:
Two thousand years behind him say
This is as it was in our day.
O how the grounded women sing

To galleried men all answering
As heaven answers earth.
Voice marries voice as if by choice;
And so the ancient circle's closed, the service done. See, there,
The man with the basket of plants outside the church,
Selling them to the farmers. But they leave him in the lurch;
They are eager to follow the band across the churchyard green
To the yellow Presbytery house, shaded by chestnuts and
    limes
And dappled by light, where numberless times
They have come about birth and death. But today they are free
To celebrate in a dance the curé's jubilee.
And now the red-sashed dancers, looking so cool and so clean,
Form themselves into a figure. The drummer wipes
His brow and begins to tap, and a young priest pipes.
And the curé comes out on the steps and smiles to see them so
    keen.
Yes. This morning the world went into the church.
Now the church comes into the world. So,
In life we oppose and appease each other.
And under the gentle trees the crowd gathers thicker and
    faster,
And a red setter dog looks everywhere for the curé, his master.
Now bright before our glance
Comes forth each white-clad mummer
To figure forth in a dance
The rise and fall of summer,
Needle-pipe and thimble-drum
Leading the way to kingdom-come.
Still oozes the old wound
The summer Prince is slain,
His blood's the poppy seed
That will rise up again
To fill the winter fields with newly-springing grain.

Afternoon, late afternoon, and the sun still hot,
As we cross the square. And all the houses have
A hat of plane-tree leaves pulled over their eyes
Against the light. But what a buzz and a fuzz
Of people are gathered to watch the *pelota*.
We can hear the *pock* of the ball against the great curved wall
Behind the church. And now we can see the players
With the basket-claws on their hands, scooping
And pawing the ball. A priest is swooping
Among them in magpie flight. He plays
In his long black robe; the others in white,
Sweeping like swallows across the court in the evening light.
Tiers on tiers of people are 'oh-ing!' and 'ah-ing!',
Watching and greeting with cries the well-placed shot.
How they mouth-in each move and stop of the ball!
And the cobbler is singing the score. The people cheer
The winning ball, and the band blares out 'all clear'.
And now the bubbling crowd boils over on to the court
To dance the evening through, until their throats are dry,
Dancing to the pipe and the little titupping drum.
And in the dusky cafés the lads and girls may be talking,
But as soon as the little drum blinks, all the talk goes blank;
A curly catching tune, and their trigger-feet are off
In a flash from the shadowy gloom,
Lads with billowing shirts, and girls with willowy skirts
Slanting along the street, linking hands as they go
In a fine kite-tail procession; or twirling toe to toe,
Weaving a wicker-work figure round all who won't give room.
And the listening moon comes up and looks down on the dizzy
    scene,
On the dancers flitting like moths round the group at the café
    table
Where two old dignified men are battling over a bottle
Twisting in wordy wedlock like eels all ready to throttle.

Outlay and intake of breath, rise and fall
Of a season, ins and outs of a dance.
Happy people. No greed for tomorrow
Greys your face like frost. O
May all your valleys be fat
With wine, and full be every vat.

Autumn Day

Going out, those bold days,
O what a gallery-roar of trees and gale-wash
Of leaves abashed me, what a shudder and shore
Of bladdery shadows dashed on windows ablaze,
What hedge-shingle seething, what vast lime-splashes
Of light clouting the land. Never had I seen
Such a running-over of clover, such tissue sheets
Of cloud poled asunder by sun, such plunges
And a thunder-load of fun. Trees, grasses, wings — all
On a hone of wind sluiced and sleeked one way,
Smooth and close as the pile of a pony's coat,
But, in a moment, smoke-slewed, glared, squinted back
And up like sticking bones shockingly unkinned.
How my heart, like all these, was silk and thistle
By turns, how it fitted and followed the stiff lifts
And easy falls of them, or, like that bird above me,
No longer crushing against cushions of air,
Hung in happy apathy, waiting for wind-rifts.
Who could not dance on, and be dandled by, such a day
Of loud expansion? when every flash and shout
Took the hook of the mind and reeled out the eye's line
Into whips and whirl-spools of light, when every ash-shoot
    shone
Like a weal and was gone in the gloom of the wind's lash.
Who could not feel it? the uplift and total subtraction
Of breath as, now bellying, now in abeyance,
The gust poured up from the camp's throat below, bringing
Garbled reports of guns and bugle-notes,
But, gullible, then drank them back again.
And I, dryly shuffling through the scurf of leaves

Fleeing like scuffled toast, was host to all these things;
In me were the spoon-swoops of wind, in me too
The rooks dying and settling like tea-leaves over the trees;
And, rumbling on rims of rhyme, mine were the haycarts
    home-creeping
Leaving the rough hedge-cheeks long-strawed and streaked
    with their weeping.

The Train

There with a screech stuck in her hair like a feather
She strikes through signals, sequels, stares, and significations
With equal squeal; scattering the stuck tons of thunder
In tunnels like tins staccato; alliterating
The laddering lights and escalatoring clatter till
At last she assonants free. The elbowing air
Ushers her on, cushions and repercussions her
In its indulgent hush. And always her weeping past
Wallabies wildly away in smokes and hang-
Overs of gloom across the long-ago fields that once were mine.
Long ago? No. The cataract still hangs
In tatters as it did. On the same thong of air
The hawk impends. Still leans the lonely tree
Above the only lake, its ageing shade
Unwrinkled in the shaking glass. And still
The fountain eyelashes a stony stare.
All's as I left it, place and pose and weather
That once was willed for ever. Once again
I look out from the train,
I see the solemn child, and wave to it in vain.

Armagh

There is a through-otherness about Armagh
Of tower and steeple,
Up on the hill are the arguing graves of the kings,
And below are the people.

Through-other as the rooks that swoop and swop
Over the sober hill
Go the people gallivanting from shop to shop
Guffawing their fill.

And the little houses run through the market-town
Slap up against the great,
Like the farmers all clabber and muck walking arm by arm
With the men of estate.

Raised at a time when Reason was all the rage,
Of grey and equal stone,
This bland face of Armagh covers an age
Of clay and feather and bone.

Through-other is its history, of Celt and Dane,
Norman and Saxon,
Who ruled the place and sounded the gamut of fame
From cow-horn to klaxon.

There is a through-otherness about Armagh
Delightful to me,
Up on the hill are the graves of the garrulous kings
Who at last can agree.

Neither Here nor There

In that land all is, and nothing's ought;
No owners or notices, only birds;
No walls anywhere, only lean wire of words
Worming brokenly out from eaten thought;
No oats growing, only ankle-lace grass
Easing and not resenting the feet that pass;
No enormous beasts, only names of them;
No bones made, bans laid, or boons expected,
No contracts, entails, hereditaments,
Anything at all that might tie or hem.

In that land all's lackadaisical;
No lakes of coddled spawn, and no locked ponds
Of settled purpose, no netted fishes;
But only inkling streams and running fronds
Fritillaried with dreams, weedy with wishes;
Nor arrogant talk is heard, haggling phrase,
But undertones, and hesitance, and haze;
On clear days mountains of meaning are seen
Humped high on the horizon; no one goes
To con their meaning, no one cares or knows.

In that land all's flat, indifferent; there
Is neither springing house or hanging tent,
No aims are entertained, and nothing is meant,
For there are no ends and no trends, no roads,
Only follow your nose to anywhere.
No one is born there, no one stays or dies,
For it is a timeless land, it lies
Between the act and the attrition, it

Marks off bound from rebound, make from break, tit
From tat, also today from tomorrow.
No Cause there comes to term, but each departs
Elsewhere to whelp its deeds, expel its darts;
There are no homecomings, of course, no good-byes
In that land, neither yearning nor scorning,
Though at night there is the smell of morning.

Home Thoughts from Abroad

Hearing, this June day, the thin thunder
Of far-off invective and old denunciation
Lambasting and lambegging the homeland,
I think of that brave man Paisley, eyeless
In Gaza, with a daisy-chain of millstones
Round his neck; groping, like blind Samson,
For the soapy pillars and greased poles of lightning
To pull them down in rains and borborygmic roars
Of rhetoric. (There but for the grace of God
Goes God.) I like his people and I like his guts
But I dislike his gods who always end
In gun-play. Some day, of course, he'll be one
With the old giants of Ireland — such as
Denis of the Drought, or Iron-Buttocks —
Who had at last to be reduced to size,
Quietly shrunken into 'wee people'
And put out to grass on the hills for good,
Minimized like cars or skirts or mums;
Photostatted to fit a literate age
And filed safely away on the dark shelves
Of memory; preserved in ink, oak-gall,
Alcohol, aspic, piety, wit. A pity,
Perhaps, if it is drama one wants. But,
Look at it this way: in this day and age
We can't really have giants lumbering
All over the place, cluttering it up,
With hair like ropes, flutes like telegraph poles,
And feet like tramcars, intent only on dogging
The fled horse of history and the Boyne.
So today across the Irish Sea I wave

And wish him well from the bottom of my heart
Where truth lies bleeding, its ear-drums burst
By the blatter of his hand-me-down talk.
In fond memory of his last stand
I dedicate this contraceptive pill
Of poetry to his unborn followers,
And I place
This bunch of beget-me-nots on his grave.

Scapegoat

God broke into my house last night
With his flying-squad, narks, batmen, bully-boys,
Proctors, bailiffs, aiders and abettors —
Call them what you will — hard-mouthed, bowler-hatted.
Hearing a lack of noise I had gone downstairs
To let the dog out.
The tall figure with his obedient shadows
Pushed past me into the light and turned
With the accusing document; all my fears.
It seemed I had for years out of mind
Owed him a sum of money and had paid
Nothing. 'Lord,' I said reluctantly, looking
Into his implacably-forgiving face,
'I would have called it a lie, but if you
Say so, it must be so.'
I do not know —
It being a dream of sorts — I do not know
If it were His son or my son
The doomsmen laid upon the floor then,
The knife to his throat.
I saw no more. But the dog of the house
Fled howling through the open door.

Requiem for Michael

killed in an Essex road accident

If dumb stone
Can spare a spark of praise
For the blind ferrule of the stick that strikes it,
Why should we,
Who have the word for dumbness, not raise
Out of our inmost heart of stone
A striking phrase or two to mark
And mitigate our parting with this boy.

It is time
To articulate grief
And to name it. To name is to numb.
Relief is in the ritual. Therefore
Prepare the cheeks for pallor. Bring out now
The dark horses with their predicated paces
And dispassionate gloom. Summon the great words
From their habitual public play
And rehearsal rooms
To mouth him to his seldom tomb today.

A thinking bell,
Like a trifling failure of silence,
Spells aloud his eighteen proud years
Of weather-vane-glory.
All flesh is grass, intones the preacher,
It is cut down, and withereth. Understatement of stone
Thinned to innuendo. Words, wind-worn to bone,
Reach us. A grief of fingers fidgets

In each glove. Around us, tip-toppled,
The leaden doves indicate love's dead-end.

Forgive us
This day our daily bread,
And remember our dead, Lord, especially this
Innumerable school-boy who
On Sunday morning cycled out of life
Before he knew it; head down
As if in a book. Screech of brakes
Like a squeal of chalk on blackboard
Snapped the last word. The day broke
Its promise to him. His shadow fled.

Long-away
And far-ago, hungry
For learning, he left a Scottish croft
For these predestined fields.
The justified skies sang, and elected silence
Opened the book of his hands and read
The man-meanings. All the English signposts
Ran to meet him. And that young girl, his sister,
Who stands there so still,
Danced under the apple-tree he had planted on the hill.

Memory
Is what we forget with.
Today, this funeral day,
Chancing to pass her gate
I suddenly saw
That gay unthinking girl
Dancing there like water,
A flower stuck in her hair,
Dancing again like laughter.

Woodenly I stood
And watched her wicked step.
What could I do but stare
(Seeing in her no treason
But only body's reason)
Until she turned to look?

And I say —
True to form and to fern
The river runs forever,
Never once does the land
Ask it to what lengths
It is prepared to go.
Each step is a reason
For going farther.

Field Day

The old farmer, nearing death, asked
To be carried outside and set down
Where he could see a certain field
'And then I will cry my heart out,' he said.

It troubles me, thinking about that man;
What shape was the field of his crying
In Donegal?

I remember a small field in Down, a field
Within fields, shaped like a triangle.
I could have stood there and looked at it
All day long.

And I remember crossing the frontier between
France and Spain at a forbidden point, and seeing
A small triangular field in Spain,
And stopping

Or walking in Ireland down any rutted by-road
To where it hit the highway, there was always
At this turning-point and abutment
A still centre, a V-shape of grass
Untouched by cornering traffic,
Where country lads larked at night.

I think I know what the shape of the field was
That made the old man weep.

A Last Word

for Louis MacNeice, died September 1963

Only a green hill
And a man with a spade
Opening the old accounts-book of earth
And writing *paid*.

Under the highly improbable sky,
Needlessly blue,
He piles the cold clay. It is all,
You might say, so dead true

To life, the meek clay turning the other cheek
To the clap of the spade
Waits to inherit the earth of the man
Whom it has made.

But he made it
That made him,
He put the word on it that gave
Life and limb.
Now to speak of an end
Is to begin.

from Epilogue

'The Character of Ireland'

Here I come, always in at the tail-end.
A good man for a funeral or a wake;
Patient in graveyards, used to thinking long
And walking short, remembering what
My careful father told me — 'If ever, son,
You have to go anywhere and have to
Run, never go! It's unlucky.' 'Slow-coach!'
My mother used to call me. 'You,' she said,
'Would be a good one to send for sorrow.'
I had a tongue in both my parents' cheeks,
Could take the word out of two different mouths,
But chose my father's slower way of talk
That had the native tint of wonder in it
To soften it; though my mother tongue,
Scots, raucous, quick, followed it hard
With hints of glottal stops.
I am Ulster, my people an abrupt people
Who like the spiky consonants in speech
And think the soft ones cissy; who dig
The *k* and *t* in orchestra, detect sin
In sinfonia, get a kick out of
Tin cans, fricatives, fornication, staccato talk,
Anything that gives or takes attack,
Like Micks, Tagues, tinkers' gets, Vatican.
An angular people, brusque and Protestant,
For whom the word is still a fighting word,
Who bristle into reticence at the sound
Of the round gift of the gab in Southern mouths.
Mine were not born with silver spoons in gob,

Nor would they thank you for the gift of tongues;
The dry riposte, the bitter repartee's
The Northman's bite and portion, his deep sup
Is silence; though, still within his shell,
He holds the old sea-roar and surge
Of rhetoric and Holy Writ.
Three hundred years ago our foundling fathers
With farthing fists and thistles in their eyes
Were planted on this foreshore,
Bibles for bibs and bloody pikes for rattles
And tombs for keeps. There was not time
To wade through wedding to a birth.
Calvin and culverin sang the cradle-song
And Cromwell made the bed.
Put to a frugal breast of swollen hopes
They did their levelling best and left it flat
As water. Winding-sheet and swaddling-band
Were one. Needle-flute and thimble-drum
Stitched the way to kingdom-come, to Derry,
Aughrim, Enniskillen, and the Boyne:
Rat-a-ta-ta, rat-a-ta-ta, rat-a-ta-ta,
Humdrummery of history.
And I, born to the purple passage,
Was heir to all that Adamnation
And hand-me-down of doom, the late comer
To the worn-out womb.
The apple blushed for me below Bellevue,
Lagan was my Jordan, Connswater
My washpot, and over Belfast
I cast out my shoe.